A DOG NAMED JIMMY

A DOG NAMED JIMMY

RAFAEL MANTESSO

AVERY
An Imprint of Penguin Random House
New York

AVERY

an imprint of Penguin Random House LLC
375 Hudson Street
New York, New York 10014

Most Avery books are available at special quantity discounts for bulk purchase
for sales promotions, premiums, fund-raising, and educational needs. Special
books or book excerpts also can be created to fit specific needs. For details,
write SpecialMarkets@penguinrandomhouse.com.

Library of Congress Cataloging-in-Publication Data
Mantesso, Rafael, date.
A dog named Jimmy / Rafael Mantesso
p.   cm.
ISBN 978-0-525-42962-3 (hardback)
1. Jimmy Choo (Bull terrier)—Pictorial works.
2. Jimmy Choo (Bull terrier)—Humor.   I. Title.
SF429.B8M36   2015   2015025750
636.755'9—dc23

Printed in the United States of America
1   3   5   7   9   10   8   6   4   2

Design by Rafael Mantesso with Amy Hill

To Jimmy Choo

ACKNOWLEDGMENTS

I would like to thank my father, Roberto; my mother, Maria Imaculada; and my sister, Carolina; and my friends Alberto Landgraf, Alexandre Minardi, Carolina Chagas and Andrea Uchida for helping me to turn this project into a reality. I would also like to thank my ex-wife for choosing Jimmy Choo's name and for leaving us with an empty flat.

Many thanks to my US agent, Alan Nevins, who sought me out and convinced me that publication of a book was possible and found me a terrific partner in Avery and then suggested to Jimmy Choo Ltd. that there was a viable partnership to be created. And in Alan's office I must thank Eddie Pietzak, who clearly keeps things running smoothly.

Of course, great thanks to the people at my publishing house who do all the thankless work that actually turns photos into a book. This includes Charlie Conrad for showing great interest and love for my work and insisting he be the publisher of this book. Thanks greatly to Gigi Campo for taking over from Charlie and shaping the book and pushing it along to publication on time despite late photos caused by an injury to Jimmy and weeks and weeks of a bandaged ear. I also would like to thank my esteemed publisher, Megan Newman, and the publicity and marketing folks: Lindsay Gordon, Farin Schlussel, Louisa Farrar and Casey Maloney. I'd like to give an extra shout-out to the interior designer, Amy Hill, who took my work and created a wonderful book and helped create my vision.

On the eastern side of the Atlantic Ocean in England, I'd like to thank Sandra Choi at Jimmy Choo Ltd., who reached out to me to show her great appreciation of my photos. It is an honor that someone with her creative talent saw the artist in me. I want to thank her for coordinating with Alan and recognizing that Jimmy could be a Jimmy Choo star. And the people who made that happen: a big thanks to Dana Gers, Marie-Laure Dubuisson, Pierre Denis, Hannah Merritt, Jean-Guilhem Lamberti and Emma Woolley at Jimmy Choo Ltd. for all their help, kindness and professionalism while dealing with my US agent and for making a dream come true.

P.S. Jimmy Choo would like to thank his breeder, Mara; his vet, Manfredo; Erica and Marcela (they have a dog daycare and take care of him when I go on long trips); and everyone who has ever liked one of his pictures on the web.

A DOG
NAMED
JIMMY

A DOG NAMED JIMMY

I woke up early on January 14. It's impossible to sleep late in the humid heat that permeates the city of Belo Horizonte, Brazil, in January. I opened my eyes and looked up at the white ceiling. I slid the top of my left foot down the soft sheet that covered the double bed, exploring the newly recovered territory. Glancing at the floor, I saw Jimmy Choo, with his head resting on the soft gray blanket and the rest of his body splayed on the cool floor, and smiled. I got up and went to brush my teeth, Jimmy Choo's eyes following my every step.

In the bathroom I began to realize the extent of the tsunami that had passed through my house. My ex-wife had left the day before. "Take whatever you like," I'd told her. "Jimmy Choo stays." As I brushed my teeth, I wandered the house, opening cabinets and doors at random. The small cabinet above the sink was practically empty—no sign of the dozens of little containers of lotions and fragrances that signal the presence of a woman in a house. In the closet my few articles of clothing swayed softly in the otherwise empty space. I paced through the living room, veranda, kitchen, bedrooms. Chairs, tables, sofas, ottomans, lamps, cabinets, glasses of all shades and sizes, place settings, pans were all gone. There was not even a wastebasket left to dispose of the plastic packaging from the toilet paper, which was also running out. She had taken everything.

It was my thirtieth birthday. The few friends who I had knew that I hated to celebrate my birthday. I would have the day to myself. Unexpectedly, I began to feel a strong sense of euphoria. I wasn't sure if that was a good sign or a bad one.

On the floor, beside the bed, Jimmy Choo launched an amorous attack on his fluffy blanket. He clenched it in his teeth and growled softly. He was hungry. Dog food in the bowl and leftover yogurt in a cup—this was breakfast for us. I put on some comfortable clothes and fastened the leash onto Jimmy's collar, and we descended for his morning walk. The warmth of the sun did both of us good. The forty-minute walk became two hours. We returned home with a new wastebasket.

While I was unwrapping the wastebasket, Jimmy Choo seemed to realize that the house was empty and it was now just us. Unlike me, he knew exactly what he felt: tremendous joy. He scurried through all the rooms at top speed, intent on occupying the full territory. Every so often he'd return to me, bump into me and then be off again. Bull terriers are the breed of dog that most intensely express their love for their owners, and they spare no effort to show this adoration.

Jimmy's joy was contagious. Laughing, I grabbed my cell phone and began to snap pictures of him in his glee. Jimmy's white body went well with the white of the floor, the white walls and the white ceiling of the apartment. We began to play, and I kept taking pictures: my feet between Jimmy's paws, Jimmy and his blanket, Jimmy wearing my suede boots. After we exhausted ourselves, Jimmy sat down next to the empty white box that had held our brand-new wastebasket, but from my perspective it looked like he'd actually gotten *in* the box. And suddenly I felt the urge to do something that I hadn't for twelve years: draw.

With a broad-tip marker, I drew a stylized skeleton of Jimmy on the white box. Then, with a red marker, I drew a heart inside the bones. It was a simple drawing of what you might see in an X-ray of Jimmy. Jimmy sat patiently as I finished the drawing and took another picture. I liked the result. I cropped the image and posted it on Instagram, my first photo of Jimmy in a drawing. The success was instantaneous. Lots of likes.

My now ex-wife and I had thought carefully before bringing a dog into our home. Luckily, my routine left time for me to care for a dog, with flexible hours that would allow me to take him for a walk every day and play with him. I researched the type of dog that I wanted and even thought about the features I'd want it to have. An all-white English bull terrier with colored ears. As for the dog's name, I left that choice up to my wife, who was a fashion design student. She chose the name of her favorite brand of shoes.

On the day we went to pick up the puppy from the bull terrier breeder, I remembered what my father, a farmer who knows animals well, had told me. "To have a loyal dog, choose the first one that comes in your direction when you get near the litter. He is the leader of the pack." I was looking for a white dog, and as it happened, the only white one in the litter came toward us in quick stumbling steps when we got to the pen. He was the one.

The breeder tried to convince us that the all-white puppy was not the strongest or sprightliest of the litter. But in my head this little white dog was already a part of my world, and I couldn't wait to see him running around on my balcony. When she saw how determined I was, the breeder agreed and spent some time explaining to me how bull terriers can be different from other dogs and how to care for one. So I learned that foot stomps, head butts, shoves and collisions would be a part of my routine with Jimmy.

Dogs choose their people, and as the days passed it became clear that Jimmy Choo had claimed me as his. The commanding voice at home was mine. Sometimes my wife and I would conduct a test: each of us would go to a corner of the house and call to Jimmy. Without fail, he'd always come trotting to me.

My marriage, though, was foundering, due to problems that had existed long before Jimmy Choo entered the picture. Soon my wife and I started talking about separating. These discussions became heated, and lots of things were said, but the question of who would end up with Jimmy was never in dispute. No matter what, he would remain with me.

As part of our attempts to make our marriage work, I had tried going to therapy. That's where I learned that I have a mild form of Asperger's syndrome. Suddenly it began to make sense that I could remember license plate numbers so easily and would walk an extra eight flights of stairs through the parking garage to avoid chance encounters with friendly neighbors in the building lobby. These habits were signs of Asperger's. My diagnosis was a relief to me, but it had no effect on the fighting with my wife. Soon we decided that it was over. More than two months after I had moved into the guest room, my now ex-wife and I called it quits, and she left on January 13.

Jimmy Choo had never disguised his euphoria at being with me and no one else. When I got home from work each day, he'd greet me with the same unbridled joy that passionate fans save for rock stars. For me, as a man with few friends, averse to social gatherings for as long as I could remember and having just ended a twelve-year relationship, Jimmy became my link to the real world. Because of him I had to go to the supermarket to buy dog food—and that's how I'd remember to buy something to eat for myself. Because of Jimmy I had to get out of the house at least twice a day for walks. Jimmy Choo imposed order on the life of this antisocial divorcé. And the emotional link between dog and owner became ever stronger.

As Jimmy and I stretched into our newfound lives in our white, empty apartment, I kept taking creative pictures of him. In our relationship I'm the alpha who gives command, but I do so tenderly. Jimmy is full of love and respect for me. There is nothing that Jimmy wouldn't do for me. Sit, beg, wiggle his ears, wag his tail. I know what makes Jimmy yawn, raise his eyebrows, growl. He will do anything to get a dog treat, and he has been known to actually do a back flip for a chunk of raw meat. When he's with me, Jimmy sleeps on his back, which is a highly vulnerable position for a dog, something he does only when he feels completely protected. When I'm at home, Jimmy is always by my side.

As I took photographs of Jimmy, I quickly established some parameters for the images. Black and white would dominate the pictures. Red, wood tones and some blue, which complement Jimmy's ginger and red ears, would be acceptable on occasion. The photographs would contain few elements. Since Jimmy is a white dog with simple lines, any extra element in the image would take attention away from him, and I was very sure that I wanted Jimmy to be the focus of all the photographs. What's more, I never wanted Jimmy to appear (or feel) distressed or belittled—he'd always be the main event, the star.

Also: all of the elements in the picture would be real. I wouldn't do any post-photo tinkering with Photoshop. Every image would contain designs I'd created, plus elements from our regular lives, like eyeglasses and hats, and the chairs, easels and other objects that I'd slowly begun to repopulate my empty home with. And, very important, none of the images would have captions. In my view, if any explanation was necessary to justify an image, it was a sign that the photo was no good.

So with the rules set, I began to take advantage of the countless images stored in my head (the hard drive of an advertising man) to create the scenes that would become the backdrops of my photographs of Jimmy. Famous commercials, cartoons, graphic novels, posters from classic films, album covers, beautiful images by Bansky, striking sketches by Basquiat, watchwords, slogans—lots of things matched the white dog with ginger ears. I also loved to draw my own new worlds for him to star in. We took the photos at night, when it wasn't as brutally hot, and except for sporadic help from friends, Jimmy Choo and I worked by ourselves the entire time. We spent practically ninety uninterrupted nights of work together. One of them was Christmas Eve. Jimmy played Santa that night, wearing a Santa hat and entwined in Christmas lights.

I have been tattooing my body for a long time, and the figures inked on my left arm are the special ones. I designed those tattoos, and they reflect the experiences that have marked my life and deserve to be eternalized. My drawing of Jimmy has been on there for years.

A dog doesn't care about the car you own, the brands of clothing you wear, if you're rich, poor, intelligent or stupid. Give him your heart and he'll give you his. How many people can you say that about? How many people can make you feel rare and pure and special? How many people can make you feel extraordinary?

Jimmy's good for me. He makes me laugh. He is a tireless companion. With these pictures I'm expressing and releasing the unconditional love that he's taught me to feel. I'm not a social guy, and I don't really like to talk to strangers—but when I talk about Jimmy Choo, I tend to gush.

Jimmy has taught me unconditional love, and this book is my way of returning it to him and sharing it with the world. We hope you enjoy it.

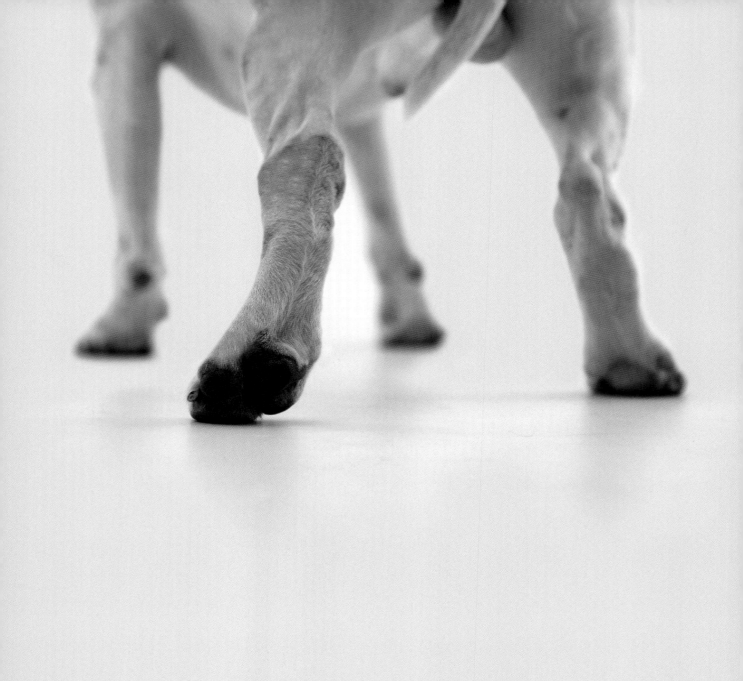

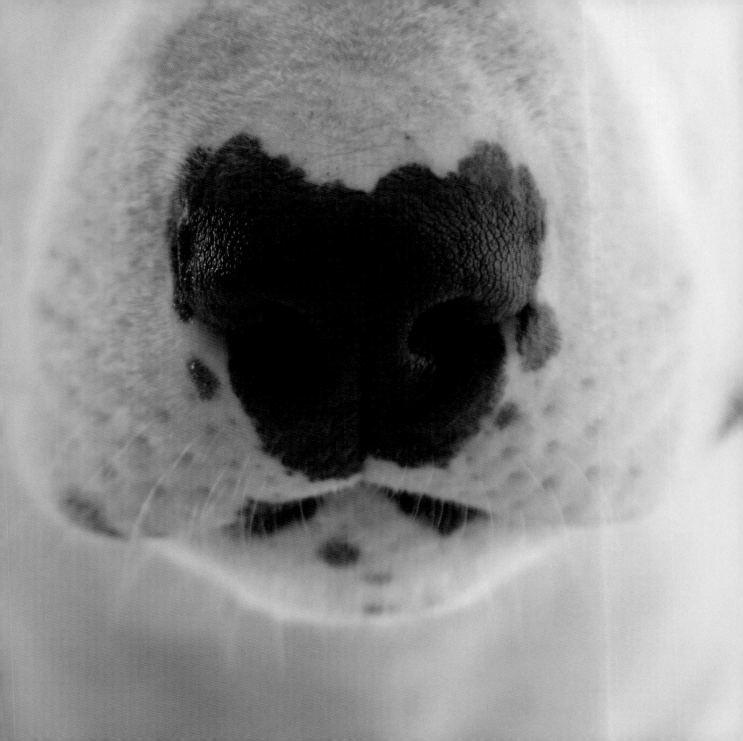

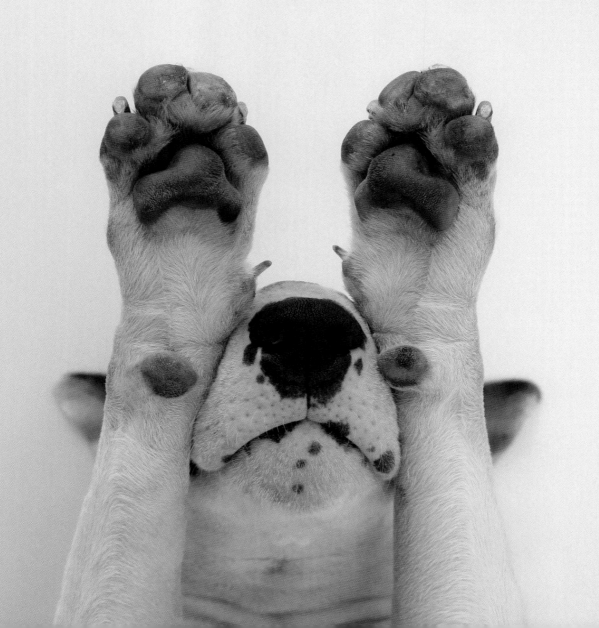

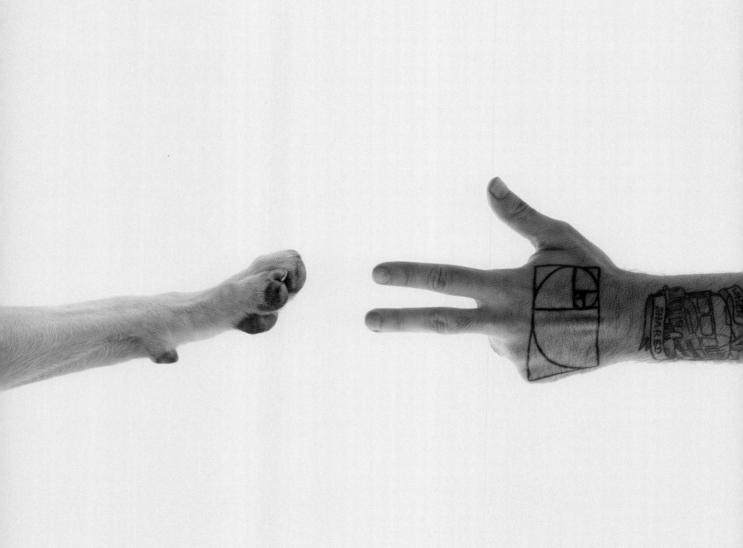

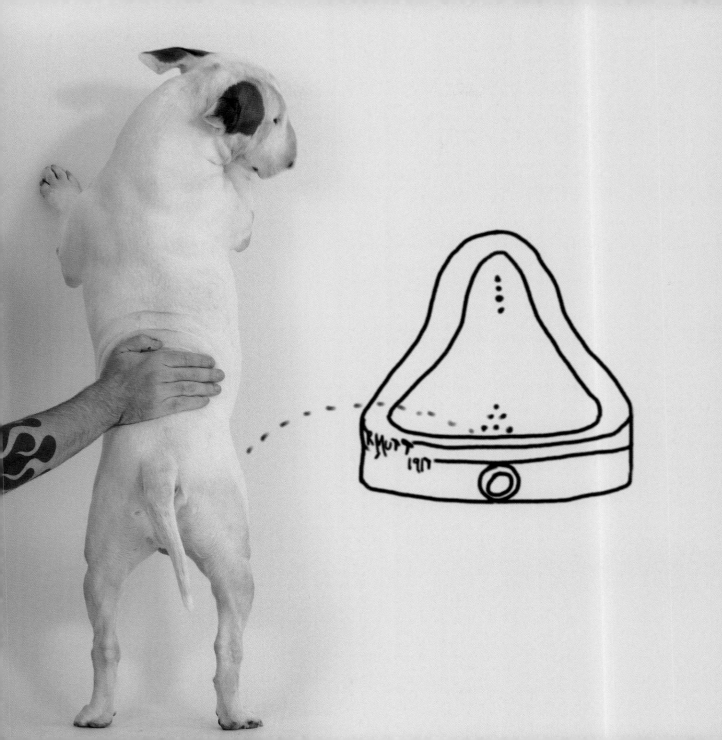

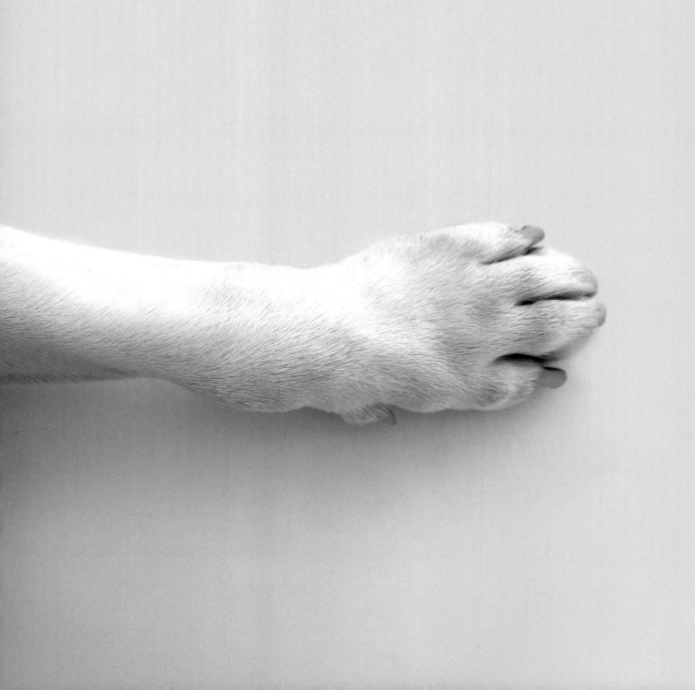

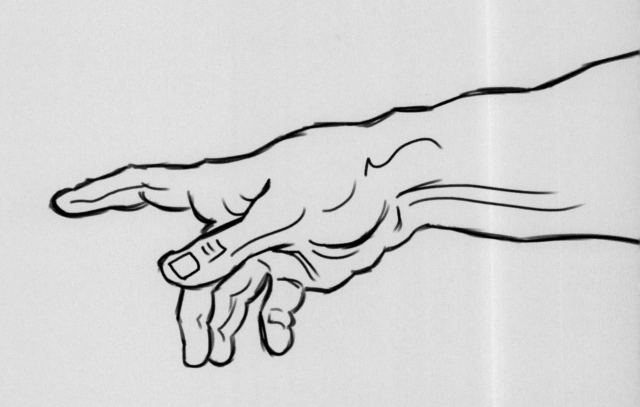

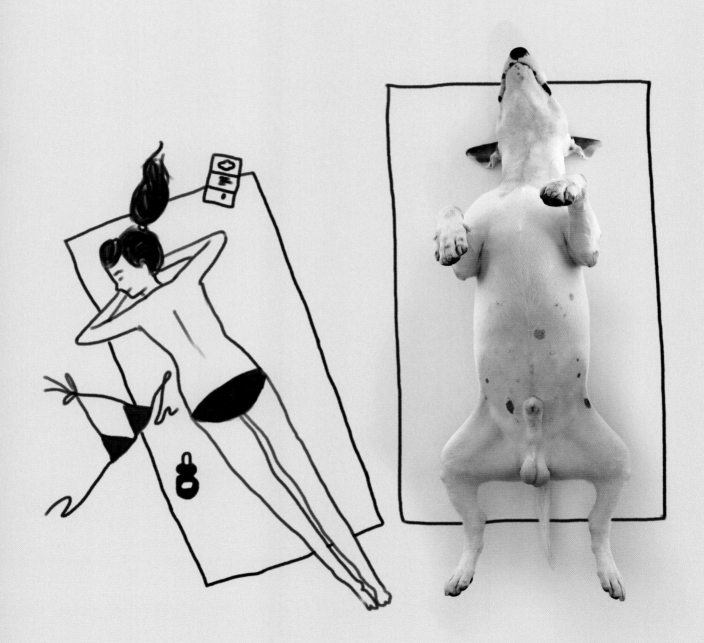

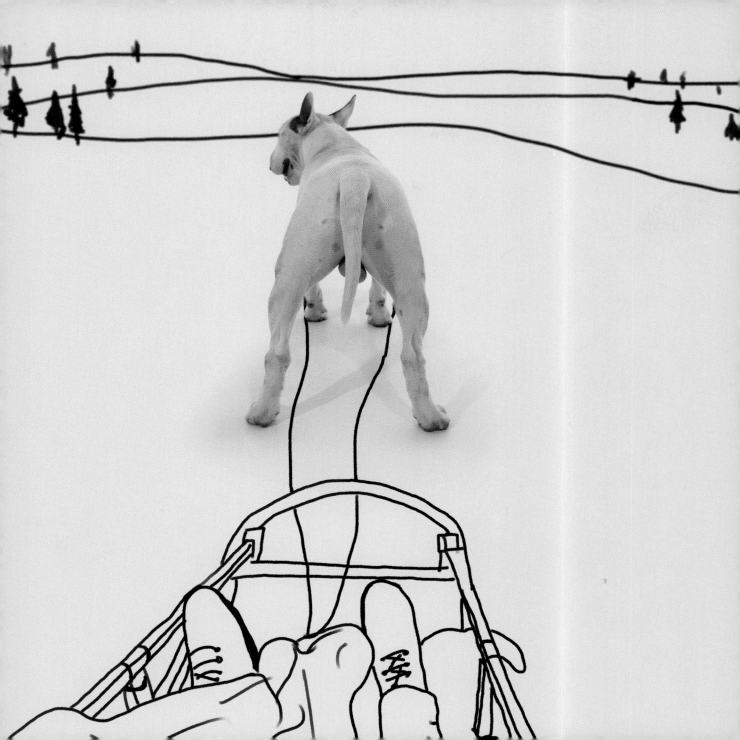

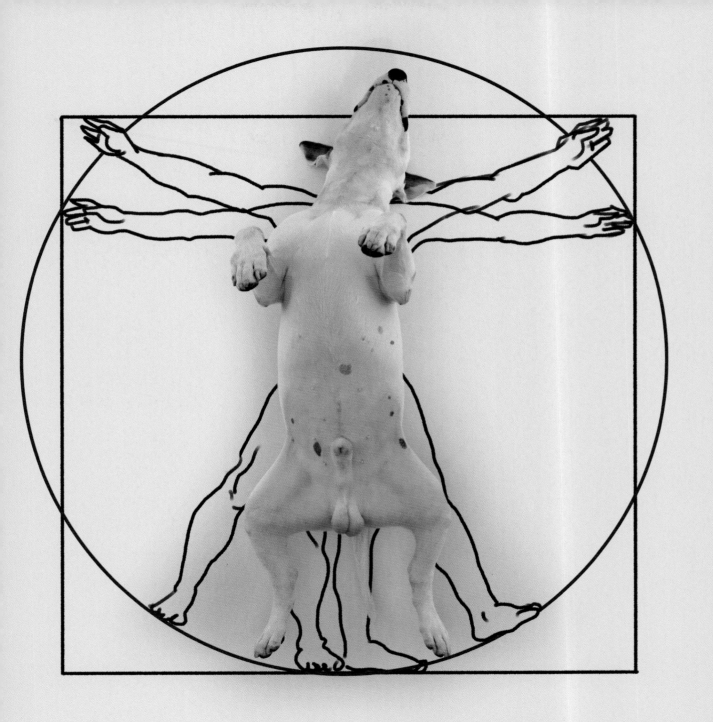

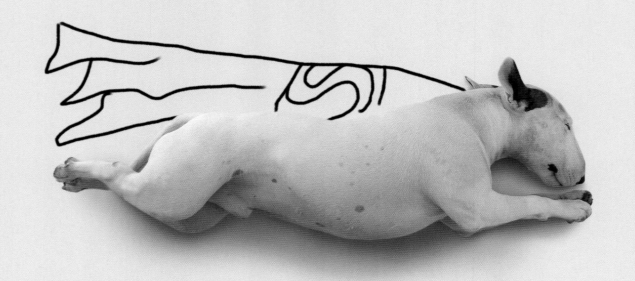

This is not a photo opportunity

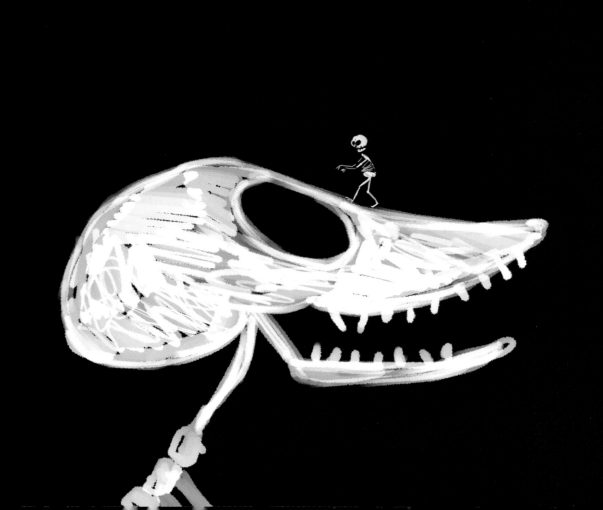

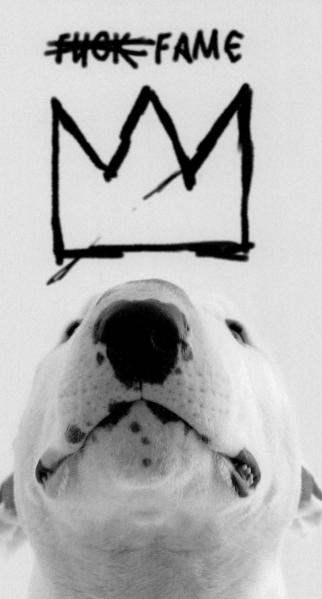

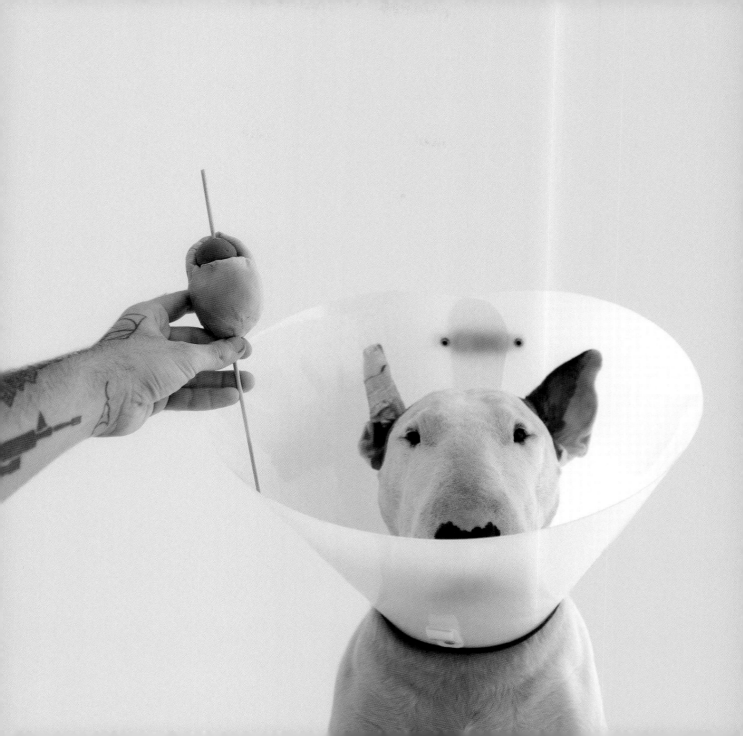

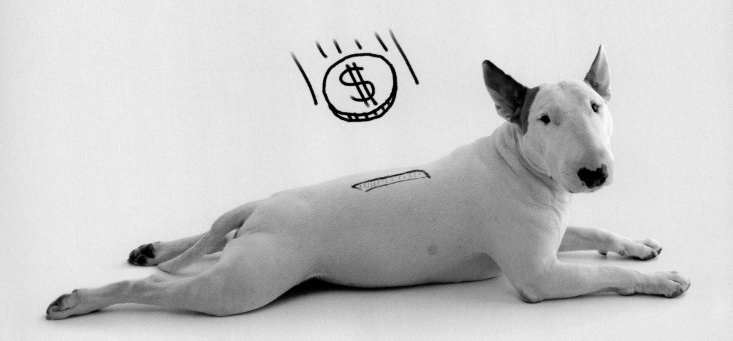

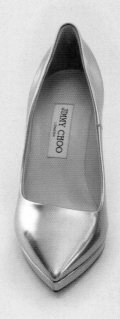

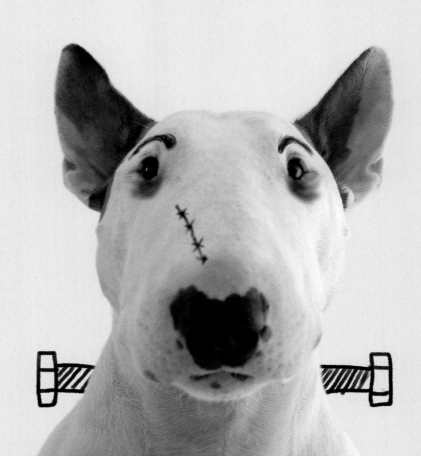

Rafael Mantesso was born in 1983 in the small town of Carangola, in Minas Gerais, Brazil. He has a bachelor's degree in marketing from Rio de Janeiro's ESPM (Escola Superior de Propaganda e Marketing). From 2003 to 2007, he worked as an art director for communications brand JWT and later in marketing and branding roles for L'Oreal. In 2005, he quit two graduate courses and decided to start a solo career. For six years, he ran the food-trend blog Marketing na Cozinha (Marketing in the Kitchen). His approach caught the attention of chef Alex Atala. In 2012, Atala invited him to be a cofounder of Instituto ATÁ, which promotes Brazilian cuisine, fosters small producers and works to preserve the environment. For the past two years, he has also been involved in the work that culminated in this book.

Jimmy Choo is Rafael Mantesso's beloved bull terrier. He's from Belo Horizonte and loves balls, bones, a gray blanket and earphones.

THE MAKING OF THE BOOK

To produce my photographs, I upgraded my equipment: purchased a digital camera, a good tripod, special lighting, and assembled an infinite white background in my dining room. I corrected the white of the images in my computer. The white of the background of the photographs was corrected using Pantone Cool Gray 1 C, the closest one I could find to the slightly gray tone of white found on the floor of my apartment. Jimmy Choo took so many baths to pose for the photographs that he had to spend a few days with a dressing on his ears.

All of the pictures were taken at night to avoid the summer heat of Brazil, which drained both of us, and to better regulate the light in the images. I have learned by studying Fibonacci's theory that people tend to like symmetrical things. If you look closely you'll see the pursuit of symmetry in the photos.